As I Saw It —

The Times Preceding and During World War II

Richard Keith Lepard

Pocahontas Press, Inc.
Blacksburg, Virginia

As I Saw It — The Times Preceding and During World War II by Richard Keith Lepard
© 1996 by Pocahontas Press, Inc.

Printed and bound in the United States of America by Old Town Printing, Christiansburg, Virginia, and Commonwealth Press, Radford, Virginia
All rights reserved. No part of this book may be reproduced in any form or by any electronic or mechanical means including information storage and retrieval systems without permission in writing from the publisher, except by a reviewer, who may quote brief passages in a review.

First printing, 1996
ISBN 0-936015-69-1 paperbound

Dedicated to

My wife Betty

and our children,

Richard J. Lepard and Jennie L. Hoyles

Special Acknowledgments

I am grateful to:

Mary Jane Brakeall for her suggestions, her special interest, and her rewrite artistry.

My neighbor Hobe Armitage for loaning to me tapes and magazines for background history.

My cousin Clarence Engler, for the picture of the carbine.

The Librarian Vickie Eckenrod of the Seneca East Public Library, and the staff — Barb Bayer, Cindy Ruffing, and Kelly Shack — for their interest and for finding the books that I needed.

Mary Kellogg, for sending me a copy of the diary written by my buddy, 1st Sergeant Charles Kellogg (1913-1995).

John F. Covert, for pictures (his special touch).

Mr. Mike Winey, Curator of the U.S. Army Military Institute, Carlisle Barracks, Pennsylvania, for information and pictures.

My niece Mary C. Holliman, for her interest and for printing this account.

John C. Dahlstrom of Findlay, Ohio, collector of military relics.

Richard Keith Lepard, December 1942

The World Situation

World War I ended November 11, 1918. Germany remained a nation but times were hard as the country attempted to recover from the war. Until 1933 Germany was governed by several political parties that survived only with the support of the Army. Adolf Hitler, an Austrian who had served in the German army, believing he could exploit this state of affairs, joined the German Workers Party, which became the National Socialist Workers Party or Nazi Party. Hitler soon became the undisputed leader.

The message of the Nazi party was to restore Germany's prosperity and position as a world power and to eliminate all Jewish citizens, children who were physically and mentally impaired, and also the elderly. World events affected Germany, and the Nazi party grew. Hitler, with his fiery oratory, became Chancellor of Germany in 1933 and a player on the international stage. During elections the Nazi party emerged as the majority party in the Reichstag; the party adopted legislation whereby Hitler became the dictator. He proceeded to purge the Nazi party of all those with opposing views. A year later he became "Führer" of the Third Reich.

Hitler planned to recapture the territory that Germany had lost during World War I. During the next few years the Germans built planes, tanks, ships, and submarines in preparation for war. In March of 1938 Hitler invaded Austria without firing a shot. He pressured the leaders of Czechoslovakia and, after threats of war, they capitulated.

At the same time, Benito Mussolini established a dictatorship in Italy. His desire was to take back territory that had been lost in earlier wars. He announced that Italy would take Tunisia and Albania and extend the frontiers with France.

World War II began on September 1, 1939, when German troops invaded Poland. During the last months of 1940, Hitler was considering war with Russia. Josef Stalin came to power in Russia in May of 1941. On June 22, 1941, the German army attacked the Soviet Union. In my opinion, Hitler was not an intelligent military leader. He should have learned the lesson from Napoleon, who said, "An army marches on its stomach." In other words, an army that cannot be kept properly supplied is going to lose. Hitler suffered through the same experience that had befallen Napoleon: the war in Russia lasted through two winters. The German army was not prepared to fight in the bitterly cold weather and eventually had to retreat.

Then Hitler had a war on two fronts.

Under Hitler's orders prison concentration camps were built in Germany and Poland. Citizens were used as slave labor; many starved to death. The Germans built crematoriums. History

RUSSIAN COURAGE AND COLD ROUT THE NAZIS

tells us more than 6 million Jews died in these camps.

The question may be asked, How did Hitler get away with this? I would like to quote Pastor Martin Niemoller: "In Germany they came for the Communists and I was not a Communist so I did not speak up. Then they came for the Jews and I was not a Jew so I did not speak up. Then they came for the trade unionists and I was not a trade unionist so I did not speak up. Then they came for the Catholics and I was a Protestant so I did not speak up. Then they came for me and, by that time, no one was left to speak up."

And I quote the great statesman Edmund Burke: "Evil will triumph when good men do nothing."

On June 16, 1940, Congress had passed a Naval Expansion Bill. In September the international situation grew worse as a result of German victories and the threat from Japan. Congress then adopted a "Two Ocean Program." However, the first ship was not ready until the end of 1942. On September 16, 1940, Congress passed the "Selective Service Act," which affected more than 16 million American citizens. President Franklin D. Roosevelt was elected for a third term of office in November 1940. On September 27, 1941, Germany, Italy, and Japan signed a pact recognizing the right for Germany and Italy to establish a "new order" in Asia. They agreed to provide support to each other by military means in the event of an attack on any of the three countries.

The people in the United States were very strongly opposed to war. At this time, however, we were still in the "Great Depression" that had followed the stock market crash in September of 1929. The United States was experiencing 50% unemployment in the big cities. The WPA (Works Project Authority) employed many people who built roads, bridges, libraries, etc. This project was funded by the Federal government and worked better than Welfare does today.

In February of 1941 the U.S. House of Representatives adopted the "Lend-Lease Bill" which allowed the United States to deliver arms and military equipment to Great Britain, France, Russia, Greece, and China to aid those countries' defense against Germany, Italy, and Japan. Great Britain's Prime Minister Winston Churchill stated his plan: if the United States would give England and the others the tools they needed to bomb the German industrial sites, the war would soon end and the U.S. would never need to send troops to foreign soil. From March of 1941 until August of 1945, the U. S. disbursed through Lend-Lease supplies of war totaling 50,690 billion dollars!

In August of 1941 the United States sent a warning to Japan that no further encroachment in the southwest Pacific would be tolerated. The U.S. had broken the Japanese code so that American military forces could track and determine Japanese Navy operations. The fact that the huge Japanese aircraft carriers had been out of contact for several weeks was unfortunately ignored.

On Sunday morning December 7, 1941, the Japanese aircraft carriers, with 384 aircraft, were 230 miles from Pearl Harbor, Hawaii. The Japanese fleet stunned the world with their surprise attack on American naval and air bases at Pearl Harbor.

On that one day there were 2,400 fatalities and 1,200 wounded in the attack. The United States became directly involved in World War II on that day. President Roosevelt went before Congress the next day, on Monday, December 8, and asked for a declaration of war against Japan, Germany, and Italy. Congress, with almost unanimous consent, declared war as they heard President Roosevelt utter one of history's most famous statements: "December 7, 1941, is a day that will live in infamy!"

Of the 70 American warships and 24 auxiliaries in Pearl Harbor, the Japanese destroyed or severely damaged 18. The Pacific Fleet and almost 200 aircraft lay in shambles. The Japanese lost 29 planes and 55 airmen. General Yamamoto flattered himself into thinking that the U.S. Navy would be knocked out in the first round and then America could not defend herself. In reality that attack served to awaken a sleeping giant. It mobilized all American resources with a vengeance!

After the attack on Pearl Harbor, Japan attacked and occupied the Gilbert Islands, Wake Island, Guam, Okinawa, and the Philippines.

These events happening on the other side of the world were about to turn my life in little Attica, Ohio, upside down.

My Own Situation

I well remember the stock market crash in September of 1929. The *Cleveland Plain Dealer* had big headlines and I heard my parents discussing it. I was 13 years old and I lived on a farm with my parents and brothers and sister. I did not know the details of the country's financial plight but I understood that we were very poor. Of course, it wasn't unusual because everyone else that we knew was also poor.

I graduated from high school in May, 1934. I lived at home and helped on the farm and worked part-time as a hired hand helping neighbors thresh wheat and oats. I had a job husking corn for room and board and 50 cents a day. When the job was finished I went back home. In November of 1936 I received a call to work as a clerk in the A & P grocery store in Attica. I worked 70- and 80-hour weeks for $7.50 a week.

Every adult can tell you where they were on December 7, 1941. It was Sunday and Betty had invited me to go with her and her family to church in Tiffin. When we arrived home, Betty's father turned on the radio and we heard the news of the bombing of Pearl Harbor by the Japanese.

Selective Service was in effect, and a few months later I received a notice to go to Toledo for

*Richard Keith Lepard and Betty Arlene Burkhardt
June 21, 1942*

a physical exam. I did not pass due to poor eyesight. About the first of May in 1942, I was called to Toledo for another exam and again I did not pass. Since I was not leaving for military service, Betty and I were married on June 21, 1942.

I received a third notice to report for a physical exam in October and was accepted. I took my oath

Mess kit. These were my dishes for three meals a day.

of allegiance on my 26th birthday, which was November 27, 1942. I was sent home for 2 weeks and reported for duty on December 9, 1942.

I was placed in a Quartermaster Truck Company at Fort Custer, Michigan. At this time we were issued our clothing and supplies including a mess kit.

The second day there, we were told to form a line and receive a pair of 4-buckle boots. The supply sergeant was handing out the boots and also doing the paperwork. I was the third soldier in line and realized this procedure would take a very long time, so I volunteered to help. I said, "Sarge, if you'll do the paperwork, I'll get the boots." The boots were already separated by size and both of us working efficiently meant the job

Carbine. One issued to each soldier and officer.

was quickly done. When we were finished, Sgt. Brown looked me in the eye and said, "Follow me." I did just that and we went to the supply room. There I learned all that had to be done to take care of a company of men. The supply room became my headquarters and I never did K.P. duty, guard duty, or close-order drill.

In 1942 a Private was paid $30 per month. Beginning in 1943, the pay rate increased to $50 per month. In February I received my first stripe and became a PFC or Private First Class. While in basic training our Company expanded to more than 300 men. A company usually consists of 150 enlisted men and 5 officers.

About the first of April, half the company shipped out to Maine and formed a truck company there. Sgt. Brown was among those that shipped out, so that left me in charge of the supply room. My job was to order, maintain, and keep inventory of all supplies needed for the company. I did not order food, but I did take care of all clothing, guns, ammunition, etc. I was the first soldier in the company to obtain an Army driver's license because I needed to drive for supplies, go to the laundry, etc. I had never driven a truck

General Eisenhour addressing the troops in the early morning hours of D-Day.

before so an instructor taught me. I soon learned there are 3 ways to drive a truck: the right way, the wrong way, and the Army's way. That theory applies to all things in the military service. Soon after I was placed in charge of supplies, I was given two more stripes. Then I was a "buck" sergeant. I became a Staff Sergeant five months after reporting for duty.

Basic training in Michigan took 5 months, and then we were shipped to Kansas for more training.

While in Kansas I ordered and received a carbine for each soldier and officer. I distributed them and everyone was required to memorize the number of his piece. While at this camp in Kansas, we were required to qualify as we fired on the range. Amazing! Everyone qualified!

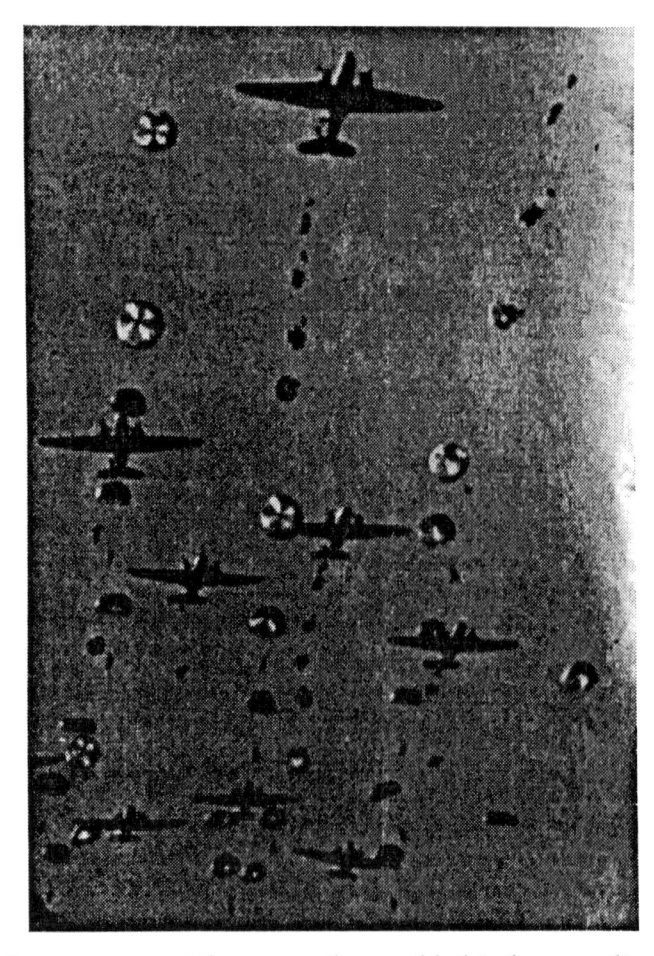

Paratroopers. They were dropped behind enemy lines on D-Day, in the early morning hours of June 6, 1944.

Off to War

After another five months, we were shipped to Indio, California, for desert training for two more months. Then it was time for a train ride across the country to Fort Dix, New Jersey. On February 10, 1944, I boarded ship at Brooklyn Harbor to go to England. We were in the largest convoy that had sailed up to that time. I was on the ship *Thomas H. Barry*. There were battleships, two aircraft carriers, destroyers, and troop ships. As many as 50 could be seen at one time. It took 23 days to cross the ocean, and I was seasick most of that time.

We landed at Swansea, Wales, and took a tram to Little Sutton, England, which was about twenty miles from Liverpool. We lived in an old castle for a few days. I needed to go to Liverpool, a major seaport on the Atlantic, to draw supplies. The Germans had bombed and buzz-bombed Liverpool. The city had taken a terrible beating. I had to drive round and round from one street to another to reach the warehouses near the dock. I understood later that a three-block area had been enclosed by a fence and left in its bombed-out condition as a reminder for the generations to come.

While in England, we lived in billets. An officer would knock on the door of each home and, if

D-Day — June 6, 1944

there was a spare bedroom, the residents had little choice except to house a soldier or two, for which they were paid.

The Allied landing on the beaches in France on D-Day had been planned for a long time. It meant a return to Freedom for France and the other European nations. The weather was an important factor. The first date selected was June 5, 1944, but the weather was cloudy and windy. The Army weather forecasters reported that the next day, June 6, would be ideal because the clouds would disappear and the tide at 6:30 a.m. would be favorable for landing.

This military event was called "Operation Overlord." Paratroopers from the 82nd and 101st American airborne divisions and the British 6th airborne division dropped behind the German gun emplacements guarding the beaches.

The Air Force bombed the coast of Normandy in the early morning hours before the landing on the beaches took place.

The Americans went in on Utah Beach and Omaha Beach.

The British and Canadians went in north of Pointe du Hoc, on three beaches named Gold, Juno, and Sword. There were 5,300 ships and craft of all sizes. The greatest aerial armada in history — consisting of 12,000 planes, some towing gliders carrying light infantry, men, and equipment — landed at designated areas called drop zones. Warships fired their big guns at the defenses. There were landing craft for men and tanks and equipment. D-Day in Normandy, described by Sir

D-Day. Landing on Omaha Beach, June 6, 1944.

Winston Churchill, was the most difficult and complicated operation that the military had ever undertaken. It marked the beginning of the end for the Germans. A total of 175,000 American, British, and Canadian troops stormed the beaches on D-Day. There were 12,000 fatalities, and most of them were at Omaha Beach. There were probably four or five times that many wounded.

THE EVENING NEWS, June 6, 1944.

    Our 3886 QM Truck Company left Bristol, England, on the Fourth of July. We landed on Utah Beach. There was plenty of evidence of the fighting that had taken place on the beach a month before. I was amazed at the number of damaged ships in the harbor.

    We had 48 flat-bed semi-trucks, 4 Jeeps, one pickup truck, one ¾ ton truck issued to me and one 2½ ton truck issued to the cooks. After landing, we drove about a mile and had to cross a small stream. Our vehicles crossed at intervals, as we had been informed that the Germans might be trying to zero in on that particular bridge. We all crossed safely and then drove inland a few miles.

    It was dark before we arrived there, so a soldier tied a white handkerchief to the barrel of his rifle and walked down the middle of the road. The first vehicle followed him and the rest of us followed bumper to bumper. Of course, we were not allowed to use lights. Blackout at that time was strictly enforced; it was forbidden to even light a match out of doors at night.

We began working immediately, hauling supplies of all kinds to the armies at the front. Most of the convoys were ammunition, and we worked day and night. It was no joy driving on strange roads at night in blackout. We lived in pup tents all this while, and a foxhole was really handy when the German planes came over at night. Each soldier and officer had been issued a small shovel.

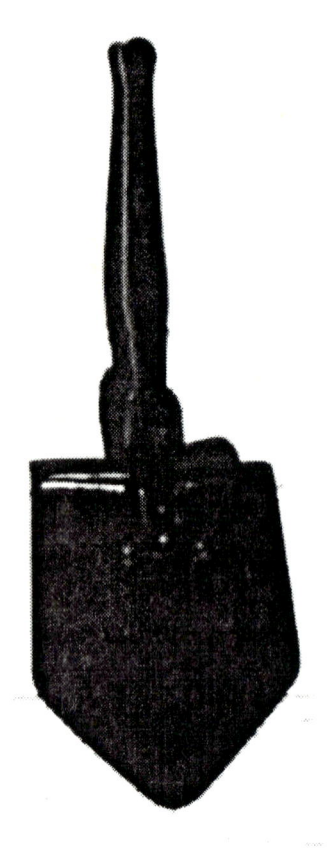

It really was a sight to see the red tracer bullets, one out of every five, going skyward at night.

General Patton and the Third Army were in England after the successful African campaign. Gen. Patton received new tanks and equipment and trained new recruits. We had been in France only a few days when we started to work for the Third Army. They had their tanks in line bumper to bumper, and our trucks were loaded with 5-gallon jerry cans filled with gasoline. Our trucks were driven between the rows of tanks and we filled their gas tanks. If the German generals had known this and had sent planes to bomb at this time, the war might have lasted longer.

At night we parked our vehicles along the hedge rows and covered them with camouflage netting so that, from the air, it would be difficult to distinguish them from the hedge rows. The Germans sent their planes at 11:00 every night. We called them "Bed Check Charlie." We did not have any protection at night until the Air Force sent P-38s about the first of August. There was, however, an anti-aircraft crew (called "ack-ack") stationed in the middle of the field, I believe, every 5 square miles. As the enemy planes drew near, one crew would stop firing and another would begin.

One night a German plane dropped a large bomb in a cow pasture about 800 feet east of our compound. All of us were afraid, not knowing where the next one might land, but that was the only bomb that night. The next morning we hurried to look at the hole in the ground. One of my buddies said his house would fit in the crater. The French farmer came out to search for his cows and found them at the opposite end of the field.

Another time "Jerry" appeared and strafed the far side of the hedge row. One night after this a German plane dropped a string of flares that stretched for two miles. The flares burned brightly for about 30 minutes. Apparently they were looking for a gasoline dump because, a little later, we saw flames going up in the distance. We were instructed if we were outside at a time like this, and not in our tents, we were not to move. I was unfortunate to be out in an open area, so I stood at Parade Rest for 30 minutes. Due to the fact that I wore glasses, I did not risk looking up lest the glare from my glasses be noticeable.

One day I will never forget is the 25th of July when the Air Force sent 3,000 bombers! They flew over the field where we were bivouacked for three hours without a break. The Air Force was on its way to bomb St. Lo, a city 35 miles east of us. St. Lo had a population of 25,000 and was a very concentrated city built on and around a little hill. Nearly all the buildings were totally destroyed.

Our trucks moved east, supplying the Third Army, and St. Lo was the first large city that we entered. We passed many former residents, pushing carts and wheelbarrows with their few possessions. I remember seeing one elderly lady scratching in the rubble with a short stick, looking for some of her possessions, while the tears streamed down her face.

The city of St. Lo had been lost four times to the Germans and won back five times. The engineers had used bulldozers to level the rubble in the streets. After the "leveling" we drove through, and our trucks were as high as the second story windows. I saw a place where an apartment house had stood. Now only the foundation was left — except for one piece: an iron water line stood three stories high in the center of the former building, with a bathtub eerily hanging onto the line.

Staff Sergeant Richard K. Lepard and Private Milton Dolan, somewhere in France, 1944.

I saw a theater building as we proceeded through the town. There were huge holes in the walls, and nearly all of the roof had been blown away. It was a strange sight to see the sun shining on the empty seats and stage.

The town of St. Lo was the "hinge" that held our armies on the Normandy Peninsula; after that was taken in August our armies moved east rapidly. As we drove across France, we used a system called "The Red Ball Highway." All loaded vehicles used the main roads going to the front, and all traffic went in the same direction. When returning empty, all vehicles used the secondary roads.

One of the cooks, a buddy of mine, spoke French. We stopped in a small town one day to ask directions. We were told the French underground forces caught a German soldier one night and hanged him because he'd been seen with a young French girl. When the German commanding officer learned that one of his soldiers had been hanged, he ordered all boys in that town between the ages of 12 and 14 to be lined up in the center of town and shot. One mother had two sons in the group. She screamed and cried and pleaded for their lives, so the Germans took one boy from the line and shot the rest. The French residents pointed to the bullet marks on the wall. They told us that members of the French underground had a life expectancy of three months.

One day while driving I saw a wooden shoe by the side of the road and stopped the truck to pick it up. I walked 50 feet and picked up the other one. The owner apparently ran right out of them. They were both covered with mud, so I cleaned them and mailed them home.

Wooden shoes found in France.

I've often wondered what happened to the owner.

I also found a German helmet by the side of the road. I mailed it home and have donated it to a museum in Findlay. The owner's name was Essig.

The commonplace activities become uncommon during wartime. We lived on "K" rations the first month in France. It consisted of dried food packed in boxes the size of crackerjack boxes, with a solid chocolate bar in the bottom. It kept us from starving and it was nourishing.

A helmet that belonged to a German soldier.

We took a bath by putting warm water in our steel helmets.

Once I enjoyed a real luxury — I was able to take a shower! A special crew had a truck equipped with a pump. They parked on a bridge and drew water from the upstream side, ran the water through a filter and then through 12 shower

Our bathtub was a steel helmet.

heads. Twelve of us could shower at one time. On nice days we could see French women washing their clothes in a stream of water and scrubbing them on a rock.

I went to the dentist once while I was in France. The dentist was located near a small wooded area. I stayed out of sight until they called my name. The dentist's assistant used a treadle to power the drill.

The ordinary activity of correspondence required special regulations. The letters that we wrote and sent back to the States to our loved ones were written on a form about 6 inches wide and about 8 inches long. These were photographed and reduced to about half size. This was called "V-Mail." Our letters were censored, and anything relevant to our location or our activity was blacked out.

In France I saw Fred Teach, a friend of mine from Attica. We had gone into service on the same day. He was driving a refrigerator truck, going to the Front with food. He saw our sign (3886 QM Truck Co.) and stopped to see me. We ate supper together, and I introduced him to our Captain. I gave Fred a sheepskin coat since the weather was getting colder. I had ordered one for each soldier in our Company, had issued them, and still had an extra coat or two.

Two of my buddies, First Sergeant Charles Kellogg and Corporal E.J. Hahn (taken somewhere in France).

    One of my buddies told me about the time when he met General Patton. He drove his truck to Cherbourg to pick up ammunition. After the truck was loaded, he was on his way to the front. He was hungry so he stopped to eat a can of "C" rations. General Patton happened to be going by. He stopped to inquire what was on the truck. General Patton let him know in no uncertain terms that he should deliver the load, then he could eat. My buddy said you have not lived until you have been chewed out by General George Patton.

*S/Sgt. Richard K. Lepard and Pvt. Milton Dolan,
in front of the Supply Tent.*

    Once a Chaplain visited our Company (shortly before we went to Germany). The men were notified that the Chaplain would hold a service in my supply tent. He spoke on the 23rd Psalm. It made a lasting impression on me when he read the fifth verse: "Thou preparest a table for me in the sight of my enemies." We could hear cannon booming in the distance, and I thought, "Here we are, with a table prepared for our Communion, and we're not far from the presence of our enemies."

*Betty Lepard with twins Richard and Jennie,
at about six months.*

About the last week in October, I received the greatest news! It was a letter from Betty's mother. Betty had given birth to twins! A boy AND a girl! They had been born on October 9, 1944. There was little time for celebration.

Chow Line. Supply Tent in rear.

As I drove the roads in France, I sometimes passed burned-out tanks and other vehicles. Some were ours, but most of the destroyed vehicles belonged to the Germans. Once the Red Cross workers visited our company. They arrived at suppertime, so they stood at the end of the chow line and gave each of us a doughnut for dessert. They were uncomfortable listening to the sound of cannon in the distance.

It was in December, while we were stationed at St. Mihiel, that General Omar Bradley visited the 3886 QM Truck Company. It was my privilege to shake hands with the famous man. St. Mihiel was a well-known battleground in France during World War I. It is about 15 miles west of Verdun. Many trenches were still visible that had been dug by the soldiers during the war thirty years earlier.

We moved to Esch, Luxembourg, on December 14, 1944. It was my privilege and good fortune to be in the capital (Luxembourg City) on the day when the nation was liberated from the Germans. The Duchess stood on the second-floor balcony of her palace and gave a speech to about 300 citizens in the courtyard. I could not understand one word, but the "hip-hip-hurrah's" from the people were unmistakable in any language. The lesson written indelibly in my mind was this:

*The reality of freedom,
once lost and then regained,
is an overwhelming, unforgettable experience.*

Richard Keith Lepard in France.

The Battle of the Bulge

The Battle of the Bulge began on December 16, 1944, and ended January 25, 1945, lasting a total of 41 days. It was officially known as the Ardennes Campaign. The Battle of the Bulge occurred because the German forces were being pushed out of France. Hitler once wrote, "Strength lies not in defense but in attack." Hitler's plan was to attack along the Belgian-German-Luxembourg border. His goal was to divide the American and British forces and to seize the seaport of Antwerp, Belgium, thereby disrupting the flow of supplies to the Allied forces.

The German forces moved at night on December 13, 14, and 15 to get in position for the attack. They had 200,000 men and 1,000 tanks and 2,000 guns deployed along a front of 60 miles. They scheduled the offensive to take place when inclement weather would ground the Allied planes. The attack began on December 16. Many brave Allied soldiers held their positions as long as they could, even though no replacements were available. The result was that the German advance was slowed. They were also slowed by the bitterly cold weather and deep snow.

After about five days, the Allied planes enjoyed good flying weather. Then the Air Force was

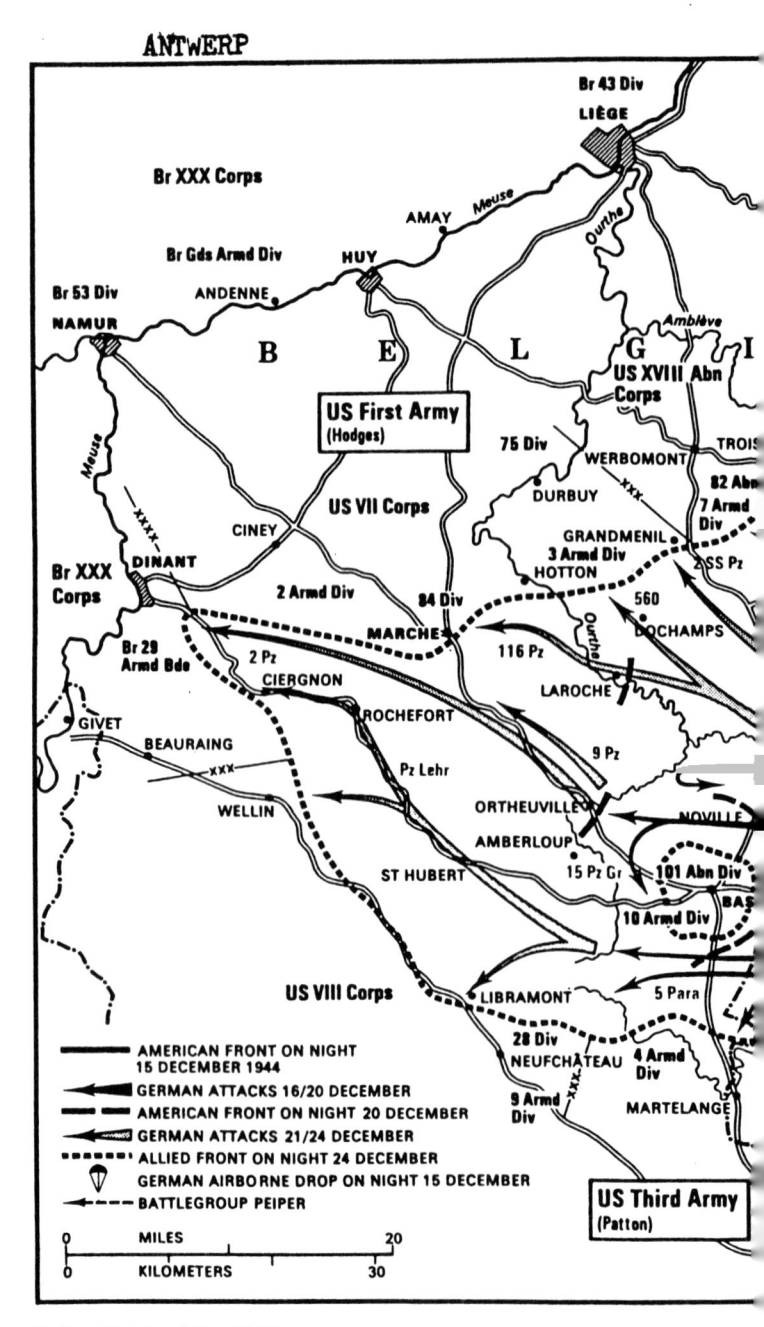

Bulge, Battle of the, 1944

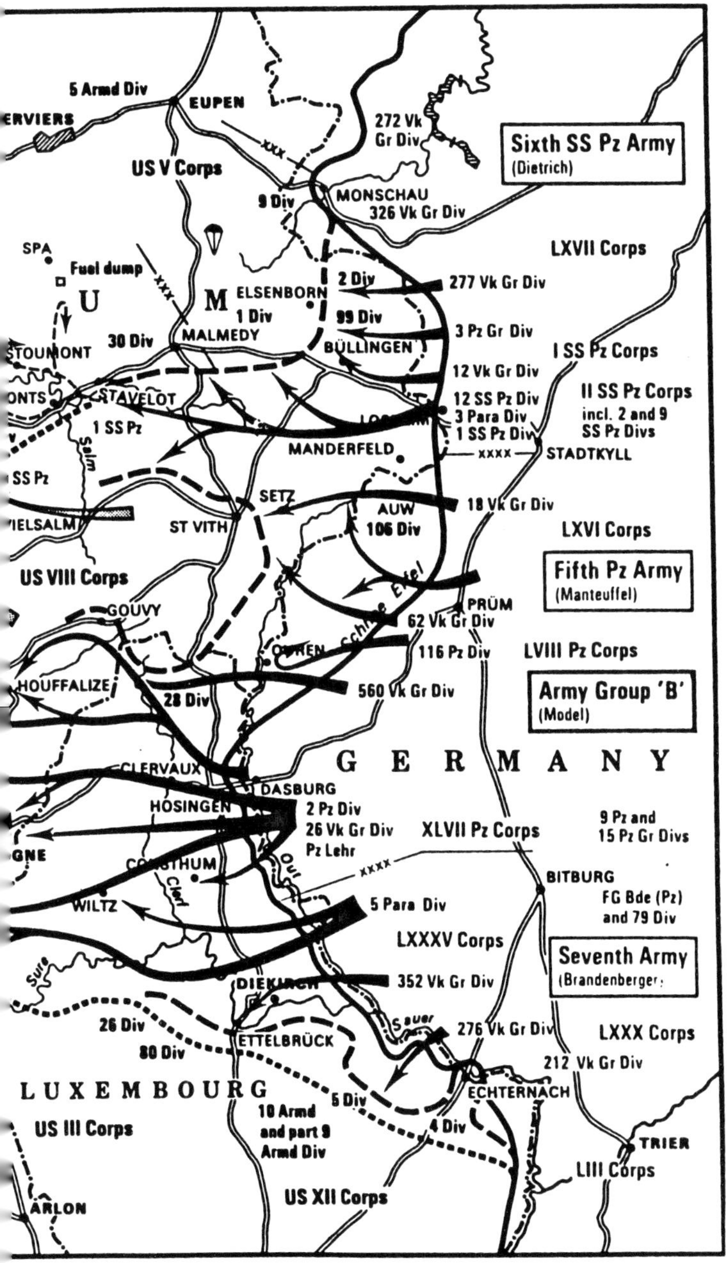
5 Armd Div
ERVIERS
EUPEN
272 Vk
Gr Div
Sixth SS Pz Army
(Dietrich)
US V Corps
9 Div
MONSCHAU
326 Vk Gr Div
SPA
Fuel dump
LXVII Corps
2 Div
277 Vk Gr Div
U
M
ELSENBORN
1 Div
99 Div
3 Pz Gr Div
30 Div
MALMEDY
STOUMONT
BÜLLINGEN
I SS Pz Corps
12 Vk Gr Div
ONTS
STAVELOT
12 SS Pz Div
3 Para Div
1 SS Pz Div
II SS Pz Corps
incl. 2 and 9
SS Pz Divs
1 SS Pz
Salm
MANDERFELD
XXXX
STADTKYLL
SS Pz
SETZ
AUW
18 Vk Gr Div
106 Div
IELSALM
ST VITH
LXVI Corps
US VIII Corps
Fifth Pz Army
(Manteuffel)
Schnee Eifel
PRÜM
GOUVY
62 Vk Gr Div
116 Pz Div
LVIII Pz Corps
HOUFFALIZE
28 Div
560 Vk Gr Div
Army Group 'B'
(Model)
G E R M A N Y
CLERVAUX
DASBURG
HOSINGEN
2 Pz Div
26 Vk Gr Div
Pz Lehr
XLVII Pz Corps
9 Pz and
15 Pz Gr Divs
GNE
XXXX
Our
BITBURG
Clerf
WILTZ
5 Para Div
FG Bde (Pz)
and 79 Div
LXXXV Corps
Seventh Army
(Brandenberger)
Sure
352 Vk Gr Div
Sauer
276 Vk Gr Div
LXXX Corps
26 Div
ETTELBRÜCK
80 Div
212 Vk Gr Div
LUXEMBOURG
5 Div
ECHTERNACH
10 Armd
and part 9
Armd Div
4 Div
US III Corps
TRIER
LIII Corps
ARLON
US XII Corps

able to bomb the enemy supply lines. The German forces advanced as far as Bastogne in the Ardennes area, then began to retreat, fighting all the way. The American generals learned a lesson from this battle: Never, never, never underestimate your opponent! The German forces lost 100,000 soldiers, 1,000 planes, and 800 tanks. They could not replace their planes and tanks because the Allied Air Force was destroying their factories at the same time. The Battle of the Bulge, like D-Day in Normandy, led to the certain defeat of the German forces.

While we were in Luxembourg, we received instructions that our mechanics were to weld a fence post to the front bumper of the Jeeps to keep those riding in the Jeep free from a "sore throat". The Germans would stretch a tight wire across the road from one tree to another! We were stopped at every road intersection by the Military Police. They asked us about the major league baseball teams from our state. I told them the Cleveland Indians were the major league team from northern Ohio. They would inquire if that team was successful and where the team's standing was in the league. It was important to know the right answers — that was a favorite method of separating the "good guys" from the enemy.

We did not follow General Patton's Third Army as they moved toward Bastogne; we would have been a liability. After all, they covered 100 miles in less than three days under miserable weather conditions. Our 48 flat-bed trucks with four machine guns, one bazooka, and one BAR

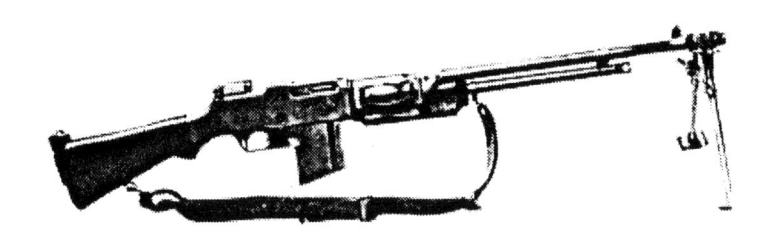

Browning automatic rifle.

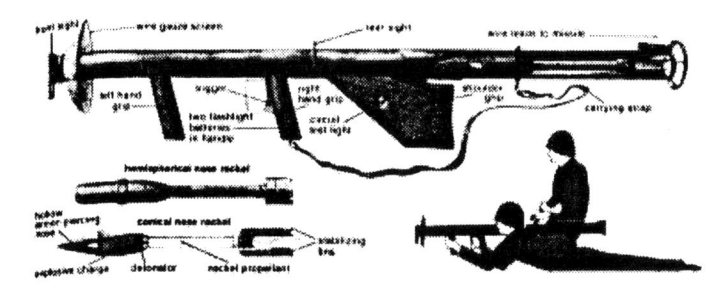

The bazooka, a portable, electrically fired rocket launcher operated by two soldiers. One soldier loaded the missile into the launcher; the other held, aimed, and fired it.

was slow and didn't provide much offensive power. As soon as it was feasible, however, we did bring supplies. We worked 12 to 18 hours per day, 7 days a week. We all learned to cat-nap, sometimes 15 minutes every couple of hours. I can still do that yet today.

We had been in Esch, Luxembourg, and received orders to move back to St. Mihiel, France. We left on December 24 and arrived four days later. I remember our noon meal on Christmas Day. It was a can of succotash! "C" rations! I remember thinking, "I'll never forget this meal and, if I live to go home, I will relish every Christmas dinner for the rest of my days!" Of course, I had the luxury of **hot** succotash because I had a small Coleman burner with gasoline. I pumped it, lit it, and could heat whatever food I had.

We moved to Contrexeville, France, on February 15, 1945. We picked up our supplies at Marseilles, a seaport on the Mediterranean. The road was open when we went to Marseilles, and the road was open when we returned. But during the time the trucks were being loaded, that area of France was lost in battle and then won again. Our choice of timing was blessed by the Grace of God!

I believe that it was somewhere in the vicinity of Nancy, France, that I first saw a hillside that had been terraced, and row after row of grapevines grew on each level. No wonder that France had so much wine and champagne, I thought.

We moved to Sarregeumines on March 26, 1945. This is on the French-German border near Saarbrüken. The next morning I began a drive into Germany. I had driven only a couple of miles when I saw two German ladies with shovels filling in the foxholes that had been dug only the night before by soldiers of the Third Army. I reasoned that the German people like to keep their country clean and neat.

When General Patton and the Third Army were ready to cross the Rhine River, our trucks were loaded with two pontoons on each truck, along with wood beams, crossbars, and thick planks. The trucks were driven to the river, then backed into place. The engineers unloaded the pontoons, put them in place, and secured them

Photo courtesy of the U.S. Army Military History Institute.

with ropes and cables. As the last truck was unloaded, General Patton was waiting in his Jeep, and the truck driver backed into Germany. It took 2½ days until the driver returned to the Company.

While we were waiting in convoy to cross over the Rhine River, three of my buddies went with me to look at a small building in an open area about ¼ mile away. My buddies left and, as I was about to leave, suddenly there appeared a small plane. The gunner opened up with machine gun fire. I set a world's record for a 200-yard dash to that building for cover.

We moved across the Rhine River on April 4, 1945, and were stationed in Mannheim, Germany. The German soldiers were laying down their arms

A German Luger pistol.

and surrendering whenever they had a chance. One of my buddies found a Luger pistol and gave it to me. It had a long barrel so we knew it was World War I vintage.

At this time the German prisoners of war were kept confined in a stockade. Each day we were allowed to select 10 or 12 of them to assist us. They did K.P. duty for the cooks, and some of them changed tires, etc., for the motor pool "Their" war

P.O.W.'s cleaning up a mess.

was over, they were well fed, and they worked willingly. One day we received orders that we would be moving, and the prisoners were told we would not have them with us anymore. They cried like children, and begged to go along. About this time we were informed that President Franklin Roosevelt had died on April 12 and Vice-president Harry Truman was now President.

While in Germany, the "Red Ball Highway" became the "Green Ball Highway". When the drivers were on the Auto-Bahn highway, they would shift the trucks into neutral, turn off the motor, coast down a hill and up the other side

This picture was taken in Germany.

First Sergeant Charles Kellogg at the Eiffel Tower in Paris, France, in summer 1945.

until it was time to start the motor and put them in gear again. This was a thrill a minute!

Each time we moved our location, the first order of business was to dig a slit trench. It was one shovel width wide and one shovel handle deep, and six feet long. A tent would be erected around it. The last order of business was to fill the trench before we moved. One time as we left, we saw a French woman place flowers on the mound.

The War is Over

I was in Heidelberg, Germany, on May 8, 1945, the day the war ended in Europe. We moved to Chelles, France, about 20 miles from Paris, arriving there on June 7. Our trucks carried the mail from Paris to Berlin.

When the war with Japan ended several months later, First Sgt. Charles Kellog and I were in Paris on a weekend pass. We celebrated V-J Day the same way the French people did: by walking along the Seine River between the Eiffel Tower and the Arc de Triomphe. We were elated because we knew we would not be going to the Pacific — our next "move" would be HOME!

In Paris that weekend, we went on a bus tour. We visited Notre Dame Cathedral, built around 1245, which is a magnificent and beautiful church. We also saw Napoleon's tomb, which Napoleon himself had designed. His casket is in the center of a room about 40 feet square. We were told that he was laid to rest in seven caskets, each made from a different kind of wood; I believe the outside one is made from mahogany. In order to view the casket, one must climb a flight of stairs and walk through a corridor and exit the opposite side from the entrance. The most interesting thing, however, is that the floor of the walkway is tilted a little. The result is that everyone viewing the casket must BOW DOWN to Napoleon, surely the plan of his supremely egotistical personality!

After our weekend in Paris we learned about all the events that led to the surrender of Japan. The atomic bomb was built in Los Alamos, New Mexico, at a cost of 2 billion dollars; it was more powerful than 20,000 tons of TNT. Scientists from the United States were joined by scientists from Germany who had been captured in France, and together they developed the A-bomb. The German scientists were responsible for building the buzz bombs used against the English cities earlier in the war. In later years these men went to Florida and worked on developing the space program.

The first atom bomb was tested on July 10, 1945. The Japanese leaders were asked repeatedly to surrender. They refused, even as they were being defeated island by island. After much soul searching, President Truman gave the order to drop the first atom bomb on Hiroshima on August 6, 1945, which killed 140,000 Japanese citizens. Again the Japanese leaders refused to surrender. Because an atom bomb could be constructed and readied every three days, the second bomb was dropped on August 9 over Nagasaki, killing 70,000 citizens. Japan agreed to surrender, and the war ended August 14, 1945. President Truman's order to use the atom bomb saved the lives of millions of American GI's and more millions of Japanese.

In the summer of 1995, news commentator Dan Rather had a TV documentary commemorating the 50th anniversary of the A-bomb. He interviewed a survivor of Hiroshima. That elderly Japanese man said that the dropping of the bomb was the proper action because, not only did it save millions of lives, it changed the philosophy of the Japanese government. Japan had not lost a war for more than 1100 years. Would Japan have used the atom bomb on the United States if they had made one first? Japanese leaders said, "Indeed, yes."

The Japanese people were elated when they heard General MacArthur's speech on the day they signed the Peace Treaty. He used the words *Freedom, Tolerance, Justice.* If the situation were reversed, would the Japanese have used those words toward the American people? Definitely not!

The thinking of some people today is that America owes Japan an apology. It seems they are forgetting and closing their eyes to the bombing of Pearl Harbor, the atrocities of the Bataan Death March, and the terrible torture of the American prisoners of war, just to name three tragedies of many. Statistics tell us that one of every three American POW's died in Japanese prisons, while one of every ten American POW's died in German prisons.

Japanese soldiers were ordered to fight to the end. They thought it more honorable to die for the Emperor than to be taken prisoner. On the island of Tarawa, more than 5,000 Japanese soldiers fought; there were only 17 survivors. Killed there were also 1,100 Marines.

It was near the end of September before we were allowed to go home. Our leave orders were handled according to a point system. I was the fifth man from our company to leave. No. 3 and No. 4 left at the same time, and we sailed home on the same ship. First we were sent to a camp named "Lucky Strike". It had a loudspeaker system, and *Sentimental Journey* was played over and over. The song was interrupted only for announcements.

I came home on a small vessel, one of many named a "Liberty Ship". We hit some bad storms in the North Atlantic, and the ship rolled all four ways; of course, I was very seasick. On the morning of the fifth day at sea, the storms subsided, the sun appeared, and everyone was ordered to go on deck for fresh air. By this time I did not care if I lived or died, so I told the officer the only way I'd go on deck was to be carried. He obliged, and volunteered the help of four husky guys. They picked me up from my bunk and carried me up to the deck. Immediately I lost consciousness, so they took me to sick bay. The medics gave me an IV.

When I recovered enough to stand, the medics told me to take a shower. You have not lived until you've had a salt water shower! The paymaster was handing out paychecks about this time, and searched the entire ship until he found me in sick bay. I was the last man on board to be paid.

I arrived in New York Harbor about October 14. The Statue of Liberty was such a welcome sight that I didn't take my eyes off it from the first moment it came into view. Our first meal was steak, mashed potatoes, and ice cream. It was a wonderful treat.

Can you imagine? Twenty long months without ice cream! Over 50 years later I'm still trying to catch up!

I was sent to a camp in Pennsylvania and then to Indiana. I was finally discharged on October 22, 1945, and arrived home in Attica about 1 o'clock in the morning. No bands...no parades...no fanfare. No one knew except my wife Betty.

I feel fortunate that I could serve my country, that I endured and survived and made the trip without serious incident. There were many times, had the tide of battle changed, that I might not be here to write this. But I do not dwell on what might have been. I came home with five Battle Stars: Normandy, Northern France, Rhineland, Central Europe, and Ardennes.

Was the war over for me when I came home? No, not really. On the following Fourth of July, I took my family to Youngstown, Ohio, to visit my sister and her family. We went to bed about 10:30 and I was asleep in a few minutes. My sister's house was adjacent to the City Park and the Fourth of July celebration began at 11:00. The first bang of the fireworks had me on the floor looking for a foxhole even before I was fully awake. I did not sleep well that night. Of course, those memories dim with time, and now I can view war movies without problems.

Will war ever cease? No, not as long as neighbors argue over a property line, nor as long as there is greed in the world, nor as long as people ignore the Tenth Commandment. Fighting was not for personal gain but to make sure that dictators could not destroy freedom in the world. Freedom is worth having, so it is worth fighting for, but it seems that those who forget or ignore the mistakes of the past are duty-bound to repeat them. You may read and see pictures about war, but the sights and the sounds and the smells of war must be experienced to be fully understood.

America is Free
and I am here
only by the Grace of God!